Love Is What Love Does

A book of poems written by

ASHTINÉ BESTEDA

St. John 6:35

Copyright © 2021 by Ashtine Besteda

All rights reserved.

ISBN 9781736992906

To my late great-grandparents,
Evelyn and Arlee Carmichael
To my dearest family,
Letitia (Mommy), Rayven,
Greg & Boot.
I love y'all so much!
Thank you for everything you've done,
pushing me into this point of purpose.
To those willing to use their life & experiences
as a fuel for love, peace, unity, and freedom.
Let us change the world.
So much love, always.
Thank you, God.

CONTENTS

LOVE IS WHAT LOVE DOES

Love Is What Love Does   3
Oh, To Be Alone   5
Angel's Perfection   7
Liberating Isolation   9
Just A Peace   11
Breaking Ground   13
Shattered Glass   15
This Real Place Exists   17
There Is Hope   19
Cold Seeds   21
A Witness, Bridge, and Dove   23
A Prepared Way   25
You Are Life   27
My Gift   29
My Art 31
You Are Loved   33
Fuel   35

Tell Me 37
Stay Focused 39
I Wouldn't Know 41
Too Much Time 43
Too Many 45
Recognize 47
Plant It Now 49
Unity 51
Good Problems 53
My Water, Your Wine 55
I Be I 57

"LOVE IS WHAT LOVE DOES"

- Mama Evelyn

Love Is What Love Does

Love is what love does, she said to me.
Like the Lord does with the flying dove,
He came and set her free.
Knew not when it was, that—the end it was
From the flesh of course
Showed her Spirit no remorse.
In the days that reigned, fleeting
You—producing wonder just by breathing
Mute—with a billion words
Present—with the lack of a verb
True gifted, you are to me
Ahead with the stars, God be
Love is what love does, she said to me
Showing me the light in love that I had never seen.
Angel's Delight, you are to me
Heavenly primed, Thank God for the seed!
Angel's Delight, you are to be
Love and divine, innate in thee.
Heavenly primed
Heavenly primed
Love is what love does, she said to me.

"Love Is What Love Does." - Evelyn Carmichael

Oh, To Be Alone

Yes, loneliness is a feeling
Something we're not yet here predicting
That feeling you get inside,
Even the ones with all the pride.
Lights! Camera! Action!
Can get it the most,
And pandemic feelings can't cut even close.
That feeling you get inside,
They say live with it—let it ride
But we know that's not the only choice
They once told me, just rejoice
This is just making a part of you
Empty feelings, just misconstrued
But you tell it here to my heart
I long for most here, in the dark
Good things, heart be pure
I say for everything, there is a cure
So we sit back and we let it ride
The good things come—[ah]—at sunrise
Heavenly pictured, the earth and the skies
I hope at night the same supply.
God's with me through all, the source
Never hoping to even the score
The moon rising up through the night
I gotta see it, the Angel's Delight.

Angel's Perfection

Angel's Perfection
I stare off in detachment
Can you see, can you hear
the face and sound of imperfection, my dear?
I've been fighting not to shed a tear
You look around, everyone's here
They bark and set the atmosphere
They now knowing, He's here.
I hear the climb, you hear the riff
Oh, what a coveted relationship.
Angel's Perfection
with no direction
I steer off in so many directions
Many testing to see it clear
Guess I didn't find it that year.
Am I wrong, am I right?
None here to accept or to deny
I later find that it's my will
I looked back and saw a big spill
Everywhere I went, everywhere I searched
Hoping the divide would come and meet me—
searched.
Unforgettably, it rings to me
All along, it lived inside of me.

Liberating Isolation

Been in liberation and in hiding,
Smiling as the earth's rising up, inside of me.
It speaks to me, divining, God leading me
Liberated in hiding, seeing so vividly
Hearing, so clear to me, He speaks
Quiet as it's kept, indeed, I am free.
Isolation confounded me
On shelves they left me
Dust collecting, but the batteries—
Still charging— how earth is kept.
Ashamed to embrace the cards you've been dealt
Look at the mess that you made.
On the shelf I happily laid
Can't conform and ain't changed my name
Earth's reformed me, and God's His name
Right on that shelf, He happily came.
Been in liberation and in hiding,
Smiling as the earth's rising up, inside of me.

Just A Peace

I want a piece
Sunsets on the beach
Though I like sunrises more
Of pure love, just one piece
Nothing less, and maybe more
One shall last a lifetime at least
Of borrowed time, you on lease—
Peace on leash—pray the Lord, my Soul He keep.
Just one love, I ask a piece
Full of sunrises and sets from the beach
From the stars straight to the sun,
Some order just can't be undone.
So can we stay in that sequence?
Within the sky, amongst these pieces
We take shape, and become the sun
Leading the way for others to come.
I want a piece, I have a piece
We became one, the sunrise you see.
Just one piece, I asked of thee
Forthwith illuminating inside of me.

Breaking Ground

Living in the light rent-free
I used to think I could never really be me
Breaking ground, as I break free
A pent-up presence inside of me.
Raised a duel, the foe being me—formerly
It was the "crazy ones" who really pulled the
   real up out of me
Flashback to when I rarely thought that
   I could really sing
Asked around but I found that they
   knew not how to dream.
It's so wild, the cast-out really reign supreme
Cast a light now and what shall you see?
A tree, Agape, being me
It grows, wisdom nurturing me.
Now cast the light...
I broke ground, I'm free.

Shattered Glass

Shattered glass, shattered glass
That sounds about right
Placed where I could see the moon & the
   stars at night.
Tell me, what's your fright?
Fear none? I have right.
Missing but what? A gun.
Fiend—off life—in the dark night
Come home & bruise your wife, right?
Your kids could see it,
Wondered what they did to reap it.
Threw us off to the hinge of the door
Seen the devil's eyes in a face before
Face about, help me get out this door
Didn't wanna see my mama hurt no more
Face of a child that couldn't hurt anymore.
Grace redeemed, countenance pleased
Sound, secure, they say we get just what we need.
Forgiven of course, that's what evened the score
Shattered glass, freed from the past
Abound in God's love, indeed, everlast.

This Real Place Exists

Early morning rise
I see purple skies with a hint of orange
Might be pink, but it looks really orange
Feels new, but like I've seen it before.
It sings of a river
It sings of joy
Wastes no time, not a fritter
Utopia, come hither,
They haven't seen you before.
Life's been rough
Hence, we shall look no more
At the past in ruins
Rather acknowledge its beauty
'Cause that's what it is…
A light leading the kids
So watch out for 'em
And watch out for it,
The thing that makes your vision amiss
I know you're sick of it,
So don't quit or stop the course.
Utopia, come hither,
They haven't seen you before.

There Is Hope

Life is about love,
Love is about giving,
But somehow it's hard to see you're winning
Indeed, from the very beginning.
So, there is hope,
Look a mother in her eyes, there is hope
Disguised, the same blood running in our vein lines,
There is hope
Our Hearts beating consecutively as we blink eyes,
There is hope
Masked and covered up by the stink of pride,
There is hope
Submerged, but deeply rooted in that sea of lies,
There. Is. Hope.
Now uncovered and trooped,
Equipped with the truth
That we're quite capable of overcoming
Turning nothing into something
Giving it all we got
Reasons to quit, we think not
We thank God for making you!
The skies painted, turning the many shades of blue.
Take a deep breath, sight ascend, exhale...
   what will you do?
Fresh wind, fresh wind, breath in, There. Is. Hope.
Comes right on time, when you think
   you're at the end of the rope.

Cold Seeds

It's been hot in the cold
But the winter is all I know.
What does the fire feel like?
Does it help you sleep at night?
It's been hot while we're in the cold
All I know is winter, never seen the snow.
The heavy silence at dinner
Or on the noisy row
Watch them plant their seeds,
See how far they grow.
But I've been built of seeds
Oh, how they'd never know.
Or if you looked, could that change it?
Now I plant, give me space and let the rain hit.
Oh, it's a tree—
A garden supply, give you all what you need.
Never grew up in snow, but the winter is all I know.
Cold isolation builds patience
For when you start to grow
'Cause I've been built of seeds
Oh, how they'd never know.

A Witness, Bridge, and Dove

A witness, a bridge, and a dove
Can anybody tell me how to feel in love?
Can anybody tell me who's really the one?
'Cause overtime I felt like it was anyone
Then no one, but I saw the sun & ran towards it.
It changed my vision
Now I sit back in patience & just listen
Wisdom speaks and you know right away
   when it's missing
Like recounting the digits when your
   currency's conflicted.
A change in course, a change in core
So much greater for us in store
Simply ran into the sun, we did
Met the dove and the witness,
   standing on the bridge.
A sound story of love, devout,
   abound in all the races
This story of love & understanding
   comes with patience
We seek this story, we seek this love
A witness, a bridge, and a dove.

A Prepared Way

Here in a room, filled with gloom, but that's
   not the case.
Thinking about my God & how He saved & not just
   in three days, but in several ways—Him.
Near sane, gave His Son Jesus to the people
   and to a cross
Bruised yet resurrected, He paid for
   everyone else's cost
See most believers would've went their
   separate ways
But He stayed, and I think I would've too.
All He gave, and our lives are just a few
Past macro-, can't comprehend it, what He knew
Yet we do...
Focus on Him a minute.
[Breathe]
Father forgive me for my actions
That focused not on love in interactions,
That paved way into distractions.
Remove the stones that I placed myself
Help me to understand Your Love & Light
Not live for myself.
Heartfelt reactions,
Works of passion,
Lead Your people to health.

Use me this one time, I pray
This one time being my lifetime & eternity
Attached to You, that's my belief, with absolute
    certainty.
God keep me & lead me, take over my ways
Accept this from my heart I pray, with all my love,
    Always.

You Are Life

Look up at the sky
The gradient shades of blue
Like the blood running through our veins—true,
That's Life.
Look at the trees that You've created
Providing shade, air, and vegetation
And Life.
A love, incapable of description
Though good diction, I share with you
If given colors to express my affection,
I could never select just one hue.
It's you, you're All
Your mere thought leaves me in awe
I can't conceive all You are to me
When calculating, I find it hard to breathe.
No au revoir,
My life You are
So present in absence
Near confounding attachment
My light, You're my star
You're my moon and my dark
Magnifique Sauveur,
Voir mon coeur.

My Gift

Well, could I really be a star?
Everybody's telling me that I will get the part
What do I do? Where do I start?
You see the love, You see my heart
You saw my passion at the arc
I hoped and prayed I'd get the part
But I've already been cast
He knows my next move from my last
He pictured me way from the past, when
   it was present
I moved through life as if I had no
   frame of reference
I met a mouthpiece, she said,
   "Do you know what you've been blessed with?"
   You're the gift and you'll be writing,
   that's what you've been blessed with—
   serve and extend The Lord's Hands with—
   your gift."
...It's me
Never had a whiff of what all entails this divine deed
But I agreed and now I see
God continue to use me.

My Art

Writing rhymes is my art
I didn't notice at the time, at the start
Writing rhymes in the church
I penned what one would call a verse
Finished the lines, I didn't know it had my heart
Rehearsed the chorus with my cousin, had to
   make sure we had our parts
I planned for us to sing it live at the church
Didn't have the beat yet but in my heart, I knew
   it could work
But somehow we never did
I'm sitting here trying to remember, but I was
   really just a kid
I kept my rhymes though, couldn't let go
Got reintroduced in the 7th grade, learning how
   poems are written
Class project, make a binder, one poem of each kind
Free verse was my favorite, so excited to
   write each rhyme
I Felt my heart expand like it did in the church
Still didn't realize rhyming was my art, didn't
   know its worth
Recited the poem in class, round of applause—
I walked past, heard students murmur—
Hers is good, wish I could write like she could

And now we take it to the 8th grade
Waking up to Centric Hits, I discovered a flame
Rising at 5 am on weekdays
Getting dressed, listening to what's her or his name
My goals began to change
I felt like music would be my lane.

You Are Loved

Young one, arise
I can see the joy & the love in disguise
I can see the reasoning of pain in your eyes
You think no one is listening, they turned
   a blind eye
But I'm here to tell you, that that is a bold lie—yes
I can feel the peace & the virtue you deeply hide
Whilst, I can see the truth you withhold—come alive
Young one, you are loved
And there are a million reasons why

Fuel

Boom! Boom! Crash!
I heard the sound of some shattered glass
Get a rag 'cause she came in with a busted lip
Made her way to the bunkbed
I laid down on her hip.
Mama, are you okay?
What can I do? What can I say?
He left the house, by the way
If only then I knew how to pray
'Cause I figured soon he would come back
But my heart would break if I heard another smack
This ain't how life goes, it ain't right
Been living life right, tryna make up for those
   nights—& even days
I remember when I saw the rage—
In his eyes, and I wondered why
Surely he didn't want our mama to die.
Just that one day I saw it
Other days I heard
That's probably why these days I just listen
You get my undivided attention
But sometimes it was fragmented
Didn't know what to do with it
A whole lot of what we didn't ask for
So I now forgive & don't ask more
'Cause peace in my heart—control lies within
And those patterns—I'm free from them

God answered my prayer
And my mother made room for greater
God willing, I'll help bless her more
   than her heart & her mind can imagine
'Cause my past & her pain fuel this here passion.

Tell Me

So tell me, what's a future?
Is it really up to me?
'Cause so many people are saying things
But on some things I can't agree.
Do I go left or do I go right?
Is it okay to have a little fright?
What if I don't do something right?
Does one mistake mean my future's plight?
Tell me, how hard should I fight?
'Cause for some, success happens overnight
But you see, I'm having trouble sleeping at night
'Cause a lot of people tell me that my future's bright
But tell me, how are they so good at predicting?
Is it a bright future that they've been living?

Stay Focused

As long as God knows my name, I'm good
I found myself viewing others a lot more lately,
   more than I should
Without a reason, found it destroying my cause
Realized it & God's been changing me,
   former self in withdrawal.
I'm seeing a lot clearer now
Vision's set, I view the mirror now
Everybody has their own purpose
Exchanging paths makes it worthless.
So you don't have to know my name &
   I don't have to know yours
As long as lives are being changed & the
   oil of the Lord pours
Anointed, we strive to see them healed,
   set free, delivered for real
So let's use our God-given gifts—our own—that's
   my great appeal.
You must know your life's importance
Be of God's use without a warrant
Let freedom be your drive
Freeing living people who are no longer alive.
So this is my urgent request,
Stay true to you & conquer every test
'Cause you will be tried, but His love, never deny
Because your life is of great importance
And I think it's about time you notice.

I Wouldn't Know

God, I get it.
Now God, I get it.
Wouldn't see the stars if I didn't have vision.
Wouldn't appreciate the light if I didn't miss it.

You allowed me to slip and stumble a couple
   times so I could feel it.
Yes, I stumbled a few times and found
   what I was missing.
Like I said, stars couldn't be seen if there
   were no vision.
You wouldn't know what hunger felt like, if
   He didn't hold the provision.
Yeah, Heaven wouldn't be so desired if
   there were no Hell.
Water couldn't be supplied if there were no well.

And in the ground is where we find our roots.
And as we look up, we discover the faithful few.
So steadfast, they stood the test.
Started to grow and now we deem them blessed.
Don't stop there, 'cause that's another test.
You can look at others for so long and forget that
   you're blessed.

Neglecting your roots, never facing your truth,
You did this all unawares,
And it's quite possible that God provided the snare.
To show you your worth, that you've had
   since birth.
You were too busy looking out,
You didn't know it was right there.

So I gotta teach you what it is to be without,
so you'll fully understand what it means to have.
Gotta sit you in the drought,
so you'll know and recognize all the
   functions of the well.
Gotta show you what the ground feels like,
so you can always say that you were there.
Gotta experience what rock bottom feels like,
so you'll know exactly how I built the well.

Too Much Time

Too much time, too much time.
Thinking it's about time I realize the devil's
   distractions in disguise.
Wasn't paying much attention when they
   said the devil was lying.
Not that I didn't believe it, but when
   he was preaching,
I didn't realize that his devices were
   so wickedly sublime.

Took up all my time—wasted mine
with a line that led to another.
He gives you what you like, but that's the trick,
thinking you remind him of his own mother.

Don't be deceived, angel, don't be deceived
   by his forces.
He'll give you distractions, playing with
   your attractions,
leaving you with a head full of voices.
And quite a bit of time it takes
'cause you can't unwind your mistakes.
You simply spend yours in recovery,
as he rejoices at your lack of discovery,
that he succeeded 'cause you lacked focus.

And now you're seated for some time,
'cause you gotta get back in line.
'Cause your vision got blurred,
you couldn't see that you were next in line.
Oh, what a wonderful time it is,
to give you the keys and expose his tricks.
'Cause next time you'll be aware.
You will have overcome,
'cause you recognized the snare.

Too Many

Too many "Gone, but not Forgottens"
Too many words to say, but we're silent
Too many questions, the first is: Why?
Why is it America's mission to see our
   Black men die?

We must unite and liberate, they say
But when's that date?
We go day-to-day, trippin' all over what it takes
Why can't we just get it together?
This can't be our fate.
Jesus obeyed and we should do the same
Tell me if it's a lie, 'cause if otherwise
Why didn't He pass the cup?
Please wake up and just listen.
This world has been so cruel, but we just livin'
Materials become our fixin'
Looking at each other, hoping and wishing
Spending money on clothes, but need food
   in the kitchen
Why did we do this to us? Does it matter at all?
You can make a difference, make big bucks
With no words on at all.
It's about time we look at the producers,
Look at this cycle they got us on.
They spend two bucks, we give ten
Tell me, in this image, what's wrong?

Again, too many Gone, but not Forgotten
Too many words to say, but we're silent
Too many questions, the first is: Why?
Why is it America's mission to see our
   Black men die?

I'll probably post this on the media, and
   gain a couple views
But that doesn't appease or address my
   concern and question
   of why there's no change or great move.
Suddenly, I'm reminded of a quote I heard
   someone once use:
At the end of the day, I must say, that
   it all begins with you.

Recognize

Unrecognizable, they claimed my face to be.
Unjustifiable, their actions were to me.
Was it truth or was it slander?
No questions asked to me.
As in a casket, I lay
with a heart but not a beat.
I place no blame amongst my brethren
as this moment is bigger than me.
I am but a servant, it was God who sent me.
Though my life was short-lived, I truly rest in peace,
as I know that those on earth continue to
   fight for me.
Diminish hate with outpouring love,
and promote kindness as your seed.
For change will grow, and the eyes will see that it
   is just what they need.
For this day will come when the wicked shall cease,
and a little Black boy with an unrecognizable face
   is one that you will never see.
Oh how I will rejoice on that day soon to come,
as you will all know that by my death, I truly won.

Plant It Now

You see, I'm fasting now, I saw it in my dream.
I know not why I'm fasting,
Dear God,
   what do I need?

A change in your heart, you see
A seed of pure love, it's in your heart, within Me
Plant it now, it's a seed
My people need it from Me.
A seed that grows enough to supply everyone's need
A seed that blooms and in course, sets everyone free
A seed to help the people that you see that
   are in need
A seed to sprout change in the areas that need Me.
The people that have been plagued a long time
   need to see Me
So I use you to plant that seed
Plant it quick, water it now, make My people believe
Now the sun's gone shine and they will finally see
Justice. Glory. My Might.
Now! Dear servant, plant My seed.

Unity

Dark mornings and bright nights
I begin to feel change, yet I sleep through the night
Awakened by dreams that captivate my speech
At 3AM, I uttered words that were so
   profound to me:
If you have love, you ought to share it
If you have peace, you ought to spare it
'Cause your kind, it Be genuine, none can dare it
Shaped Divine, within its time and such rareness
Most swift in its prime, lest we be careless
Many arraigned and detained, thus we must
   share this.
Given in love, this is truth
And proof reigns synonymous
We stand together in thine dew
To see the sun shine, as I knew
Unity, at core, must be true
Yet, it begins with me and you.

Good Problems

Everybody's got a problem
Yours no greater than mine
Maybe it's what keeps us grounded
We chip one bit off at a time.
So don't think I'm perfect
That's perfectly fine
As this problem sits & ferments
Just as aged wine.
I'm grounded, progressing with mine
As I move forward,
Chipping off one bit at a time.
No blood atones—conquering
As my Savior, divine.
Thus, I remain grounded.
God, take care of mine.

My Water, Your Wine

Oh, but this wine is good
Helps others as much as it should
I casted doubt, hoping for another route
Hiding my problems, some others couldn't
   live without.
My water is your wine, in some cases
So I sit & ferment—go through—lest we trade places
What I did—you won't do—with a couple wine sips
You'll know what I knew, right after it ferments.
Aged wine, I went through so you wouldn't have to
Aged wine, a ground brew to easily pass through
My water may be your wine
What I went through, you view as new.
So here's this cup, yes, I'll tell you all about
   my problems
Tastes like wine, but it's my water 'cause I already
   solved 'em.

I Be I

Open skies
To Heaven's sunrise
I hear the demise
of the lost, here in disguise
Blinded and wounded inside
I hear tears and their cries
Cannot I Be I?
A Silent womb, a humble cry
Not an eye for an eye
Nor a blind man in the light
Shuttered wounds and ample light
To false privileges, I now deny
It's time that I Be I
Who hears the cry in the silent night?
Who knows the love hidden in the fright?
A marveled awe, a tattered tale
A truth speaks, a living well
Far from mine, I cannot tell
A broken life can make it well
A hampered story, I now unveil
Can I Be I, and We Be Well?
Over and over
I hear them say:
Can I be I to lead the way?
A broken question, a sovereign deed
Framed from a man, a man with needs
Raw imperfection, you are
If you be I, you won't go far

Heaven's nigh, you reign subpar
As I Be I, thy reign is far
Come now and test it
Come now, arrested
From an eye to I
Alike, from the inside
Profane in thy name
Statuses—now constrained
You fly, you fly high
As I Be I.
And oh, none will deny
None can turn aside
A true I for an eye
As I Be I.
Welcome now, welcome all
A sovereign problem, sound resolve
You hear now, you hear all
I hear the sound, you hear the call
A true I for an eye
A true no one shall deny
You go forth, none come nigh
As I Be I.
A sovereign deploy, a heavenly joy
Your life, it Be Mine, no need to decoy
As you take flight and rise
You rise before the eye,
The eye created by The I
The I no one can deny
You take flight, you rise high
As I Be I.

Turn to the blindside,
To the man with the pride
You are but an eye
Let I Be I.
And to the one without hope
And to the one with no scope
Life reigns small in thine eye
Thus, let I Be I.
You are set, you are ready
No weight moves you from steady
Nor leaves you lost, away from light
Benefits of I Being I.
This is rich, this is life
A life lived, One with I
A life lived before the eye
As I Be I.
Watch what you have inside
What is not seen by the eye
No reason is there to hide
As thine I Be like Mine.

ABOUT THE AUTHOR

Ashtiné Besteda was born in Virginia Beach, Virginia, and raised in Daphne, Mobile, and Spanish Fort, Alabama. In addition to her book of poetry, *Love Is What Love Does*, she has written and recorded songs, among them "Hard to Feel," "Mute," and "Don't Text."